D1408155

JUNIOR
BIOGRAPHIES

HILLARY CLINTON

POLITICIAN AND ACTIVIST

Portia Summers

E

Enslow Publishing
101 W. 23rd Street
Suite 240
New York, NY 10011
USA

enslow.com

WORDS TO KNOW

advocate A person who fights on behalf of a person or cause.

campaign The events before an election when candidates try to get people to vote for them.

candidate A person who is running for an office.

custody The right to take care of a child.

economy A country's money and how it is used.

Electoral College People from each state who choose the president based on whom the people in each state voted for.

migrant Moving from place to place, often looking for work or food.

political science The study of politics and government.

postgraduate A degree or education earned after a four-year college degree.

strike Stopping work because of unfair treatment.

textile Cloth.

vaccine A shot that protects someone from disease.

CONTENTS

Hillary Rodham Clinton

Hillary Rodham Clinton was born on October 26, 1947, in Chicago, Illinois. Her father ran a successful **textile** company. Hillary was the oldest of three children. She helped take care of her two younger brothers, Hugh and Tony. When she was three years old, her family moved to Park Ridge, Illinois. She did well in school, and she was a Girl Scout.

EDUCATION

In high school, Hillary was a member of the National Honor Society, the student

When Hillary was young, she thought about being an astronaut. She wrote to NASA, but they told her that women were not allowed in the space program.

Hillary's high school yearbook photo, 1965

council, and the school newspaper. She was elected vice president of her junior class, but she lost the race for class president in her senior year. She graduated near the top of her class in 1965.

That fall, Hillary started at Wellesley College, where she studied political science. She became very involved in politics at school. In 1968, Hillary was elected president of the student government. After Martin Luther King Jr. was killed that

Hillary Says:
"Take criticism seriously, but not personally."

year, she organized a two-day student **strike**. She believed the school should have more black students and teachers.

Hillary graduated with honors in 1969. It was a special day. She was the first Wellesley student to make a speech at graduation. The speech got a lot of attention, including an article in *Life* magazine. She was also interviewed on a talk show. It was Hillary's first step into the spotlight of politics.

Hillary at Wellesley

CHAPTER 2
AN INDEPENDENT WOMAN

In 1969, Hillary started at Yale Law School. While she was at law school, she worked with child abuse cases and gave free law advice to the poor. She also learned a lot about the problems of **migrant** workers, like housing, health care, and education. Her years as a law student made her realize that she wanted to help people in need.

BILL CLINTON

In 1971, Hillary began dating William Jefferson Clinton. Bill, who was from Arkansas, was also a student at Yale. The two met in class. Bill couldn't stop looking at Hillary. Finally, she walked over and introduced herself.

Hillary Says:

"Always aim high, work hard, and care deeply about what you believe in."

An early photo of Hillary and Bill

During that summer, Hillary went to California to work child **custody** cases. Bill changed his own summer plans and followed her to California. He asked Hillary to marry him after they graduated from Yale in 1973.

In 1974, Bill and Hillary moved to Fayetteville, Arkansas. The next year they got married in their living room. Hillary decided she would not take Bill's last name. She became one of only two female professors at the law school at the University of Arkansas, Fayetteville.

FIRST LADY OF ARKANSAS

Hillary was very busy as a teacher and a lawyer. She fought for the rights of women and children in court. In 1977, she started the Arkansas **Advocates** for Children and Families.

Hillary was part of the team of lawyers bringing impeachment charges against President Richard Nixon in 1974.

In 1978, Bill Clinton was elected governor of Arkansas. Soon after, Hillary had her own success when she became the first female partner at Rose Law Firm. On February 27, 1980, she

Hillary and Bill with baby Chelsea, March 3, 1980

gave birth to daughter Chelsea. That same year, Bill lost the election for a second term as governor. But he tried again in 1982, and he was voted back into office.

From 1980 until Bill Clinton was elected president in 1992, Hillary made more money than her husband.

Chapter 3
First Lady of the United States and More

Hillary kept working while her husband was governor. She began using Bill's last name and called herself Hillary Rodham Clinton. As a lawyer, she tried to improve education by making sure classrooms did not have too many students and teachers were well trained. She also started a state program that helped parents prepare their children for school.

Active First Lady

The year 1992 was a big one for the Clintons. Bill Clinton ran for president of the United States and won. The

Hillary Says:
"All of us have to recognize that we owe our children more than we have been giving them."

Hillary and Bill dance at his inaugural ball in 1993.

In 1997, Hillary won a Grammy for her recording of her book *It Takes a Village.*

family moved into the White House. Hillary was the first First Lady of the United States to have a **postgraduate** degree. She was also the first to have her own career before her husband became president. Hillary set up her own office in the White House. Her husband gave her the big job of changing the health care system. She was busier than ever.

President Clinton was reelected in 1996. Hillary continued her work in health care and children's rights. She helped make sure children had health insurance and that they got the **vaccines** they needed. She also helped orphans with special needs get into foster care. She believes this was one of the most important things she did as First Lady.

First Lady Hillary speaks at a meeting about women's leadership.

CAPITOL HILL AND THE WHITE HOUSE

Toward the end of the Clintons' time in the White House, Hillary decided to run for US Senate for the state of New York. She became a senator in 2000. Hillary fought hard for the recovery of Washington, DC, and New York City after the 9/11 terrorist attacks. She supported sending troops into Afghanistan.

Hillary was reelected in 2006. But in 2007, she found a new goal. She would run for president of the United States. In order to be the **candidate** for the Democratic Party, she had to run against Senator Barack Obama. Hillary lost, but she gained a new role: secretary of state.

SECRETARY OF STATE

Being secretary of state was not an easy job. The country was at war, and the **economy** was struggling. Many people

Secretary of State Clinton meets with Indian prime minister Singh in 2009.

were having a difficult time. Hillary had to work with many different countries while she tried to do what was best for the United States. She visited 112 countries while she was in office, the most of any secretary of state. Hillary stepped down from her role in 2012.

Hillary's next move was not a surprise to the people who knew her. She wanted to run for president again. In 2016, after a tough **campaign**, Hillary won the nomination for the Democratic Party. She was the first woman to become the candidate for a major political party.

Donald Trump, a businessman from New York, became the Republican Party nominee. He had no experience in politics. Many people liked this fact. But Donald said many things that offended people. Hillary had the support of her party as well as the Obamas. She believed she had a good chance to win.

During Hillary's 2016 campaign, her voters used the slogan "I'm With Her."

Hillary accepts the presidential nomination at the 2016 Democratic National Convention.

Hillary ran a strong campaign. She was well-prepared when she faced Donald Trump in the debates. She discussed her plans for health care, jobs, and education. Many polls predicted that she would win. But on November 8, 2016, Hillary did not get enough votes in the Electoral College to become president. Even though more people voted for Hillary, she did not win enough states.

THE FIGHT GOES ON

Over her long career, Hillary has helped many people who did not have a voice. She has worked for equality for

Hillary Says:

"To all the little girls out there...never doubt that you are valuable and powerful and deserving of every chance and opportunity in the world to pursue and achieve your own dreams."

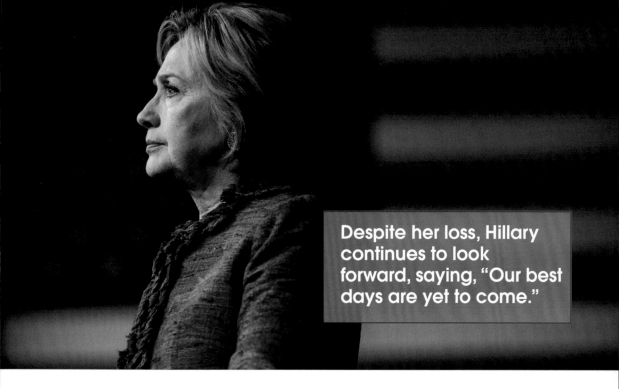

Despite her loss, Hillary continues to look forward, saying, "Our best days are yet to come."

everyone and has become a role model for women of all ages. Even though she lost the battle to be president, we can be sure that Hillary Clinton will not stop fighting.

1947—Hillary Rodham Clinton is born in Chicago, Illinois, on October 26.

1965—Begins studying political science at Wellesley College.

1969—Enters law school at Yale University.

1971—Meets Bill Clinton.

1973—Graduates from Yale.

1974—Works as an attorney for the Children's Defense Fund

1975—Marries Bill Clinton, moves to Arkansas, begins teaching at University of Arkansas.

1979—Becomes partner at Rose Law Firm in Little Rock.

1980—Daughter Chelsea is born.

1983—Hillary becomes head of the Arkansas Education Standards Committee.

1992—Bill Clinton is elected president of the United States.

1993—Hillary is appointed head of the task force on national health care reform.

2000—Becomes a US senator representing New York.

2006—Wins reelection to Senate.

2008—Runs against Barack Obama for Democratic nomination for president and loses.

2009—Becomes secretary of state.

2013—Resigns as secretary of state.

2015—Announces bid for president of the United States.

2016—Loses presidential race to Donald Trump; continues work with Clinton Foundation and other charities.

BOOKS

Corey, Shana. *Hillary Clinton: The Life of a Leader.* New York, NY: Random House, 2016.

Furi-Perry, Ursula. *Constitutional Law for Kids: Discovering the Rights and Privileges Granted by the U.S. Constitution.* Washington, DC: The American Bar Association, 2014.

Reis, Ronald A. *The US Congress for Kids: Over 200 Years of Lawmaking, Deal-Breaking, and Compromising.* Chicago, IL: Chicago Press Review, 2014.

WEBSITES

Ben's Guide
bensguide.gpo.gov
Ben Franklin will guide you through American government and politics.

Time for Kids
www.timeforkids.com/news/meet-hillary-clinton/415951
Learn more about Hillary Clinton.

INDEX

Dedication: The author would like to thank all of the women who have broken through glass ceilings for the women that follow them and to encourage young women and girls to continue to do so.

Published in 2018 by Enslow Publishing, LLC
101 W. 23rd Street, Suite 240, New York, NY 10011

Library of Congress Cataloging-in-Publication Data
Names: Summers, Portia, author.
Title: Hillary Clinton : politician and activist / Portia Summers.
Description: New York : Enslow Publishing, 2018. | Series: Junior biographies | Includes bibliographical references and index.
Identifiers: LCCN 2017003108 | ISBN 9780766086708 (library-bound) | ISBN 9780766087859 (paperback) | ISBN 9780766087866 (6-pack)
Subjects: LCSH: Clinton, Hillary Rodham—Juvenile literature. | Presidential candidates—United States—Biography—Juvenile literature. | Women presidential candidates—United States—Biography—Juvenile literature. | Cabinet officers—United States—Biography—Juvenile literature. | Women cabinet officers—United States—Biography—Juvenile literature. | United States. Department of State—Biography—Juvenile literature. | United States. Congress. Senate—Biography—Juvenile literature. | Legislators—United States—Biography—Juvenile literature. | Women legislators—United States—Biography—Juvenile literature. | Presidents' spouses—United States—Biography—Juvenile literature.
Classification: LCC E887.C55 S86 2018 | DDC 324.092 [B]—dc23
LC record available at https://lccn.loc.gov/2017003108

Printed in the United States of America

To Our Readers: We have done our best to make sure all websites in this book were active and appropriate when we went to press. However, the author and the publisher have no control over and assume no liability for the material available on those websites or on any websites they may link to. Any comments or suggestions can be sent by email to customerservice@enslow.com.

Photo Credits: Cover, p. 1 Ethan Miller/Getty Images; p. 4 Win McNamee/Getty Images; pp. 6, 9 Wellesley College/Sygma/Getty Images; p. 7 Wellesley College Archives/REUTERS/Newscom; p. 10 David Hume Kennerly/3rd Party - Misc/Getty Images; p. 11 © AP Images; p. 13 Jeffrey Markowitz/Sygma/Getty Images; p. 15 Mark Wilson/Hulton Archive/Getty Images; p. 17 Paul J. Richards/AFP/Getty Images; p. 19 Chip Somodevilla/Getty Images; p. 21 The Washington Post/Getty Images; pp. 2, 3, 22, 23, 24 (curves graphic) Alena Kazlouskaya/Shutterstock.com; interior pages (stars & stripes) Darina Bagan/Shutterstock.com.